Finding the
EXTRA IN YOUR ORDINARY

SCOTT DARYL ANDERSON

Edited by Pat Falting

ISBN 978-1-64349-454-8 (paperback)
ISBN 978-1-64349-455-5 (digital)

Copyright © 2018 by Scott Daryl Anderson

All rights reserved. No part of this publication may be reproduced, distributed, or transmitted in any form or by any means, including photocopying, recording, or other electronic or mechanical methods without the prior written permission of the publisher. For permission requests, solicit the publisher via the address below.

Christian Faith Publishing, Inc.
832 Park Avenue
Meadville, PA 16335
www.christianfaithpublishing.com

Printed in the United States of America

Dedication

I dedicate this book to everyone who has ever felt that their life has not mattered all that much. This idea is simply a lie from an enemy who likes you to be stuck in the rut of wrong perspective, unmotivated by believing that you are not the champion that God has destined you to be.

To Nahowan Saxon, my son, whose conversation at a Newk's Deli birthed this book. Thank you for inspiring me and making me so angry at what modern culture is telling people that I wrote this book with you in mind from start to finish. You are far more successful than you have ever imagined and I am very proud of you!

To my amazing wife Stephanie—you truly are the other side of me. I continue to be surprised by the gift God has given me in you, our marriage and our friendship. I love you!

To Elijah, Macee, Abraham and Shadrach—being your dad is one of my all time greatest achievements and I never take the responsibility lightly. Have I told you I love you today?

Contents

Introduction 9
1 Unreal Expectations 17
    a. What Most People's Lives Look Like 21
    b. Why Our Culture Wants More 25
2 The Average Life of People 33
    c. What Is Truly Important ...37
    d. How to Balance Our Drive over Our Destiny 43

3 Faithful in the Little 51
    e. Being Consistent—
       Being the Master of
       the Mundane 58
4 When God Puts His
   Extra into Your Ordinary 65
5 Faithful in the Big 87
    f. When the Little
       Becomes Big 90
    g. Destiny and the
       Devil Is in the Details 96
6 The Greatest of These Is Love 99
    h. Love Is Spelled T-I-M-E ... 101
    i. Do They Know? 104
7 It's Who You Build, Not
   What You Build 109
    j. Contentment 120

Aftermath..................................137
Endnotes....................................139

Introduction

In the movie *The Hobbit,* Gandalf is meeting with the elvin King Elrond; Galadriel, Lady of Light; and Saruman the White. They are discussing the outbreak of war that is coming to Middle Earth. They are discussing the looming darkness of hopelessness that is taking over. And they are discussing that none of them have the power to overthrow the enemy that awaits them. Saruman in particular is obsessed with power, resourcefulness, and superstars. He believes that there are not enough talented people to win the impending war.

As Saruman rambles about the impending disaster, an interesting sidebar begins to play out. Galadriel and Gandalf begin to have a private conversation telepathically while Saruman is speaking. Gandalf says something most remarkable in this exchange of thoughts; in fact, his words have become the very backbone of this book. I want you to truly focus on these words because many of us feel just as these four beings felt. We feel as if our best efforts are never enough, that what we are facing is too much for us, and that the idea of winning is a hopeless fantasy.

Galadriel asks Gandalf about Bilbo, the hobbit. She is curious why Gandalf has chosen a halfling to help in these dire circumstances, a pint-sized solution to tackle an enormous problem. Gandalf's answer is profound:

> Saruman believes it is only great power that can hold evil in check, but that is not what I have found.

> It is the small things, everyday deeds of ordinary folk that keeps the darkness at bay. Small acts of kindness and love. Why Bilbo Baggins? Perhaps because I am afraid, and he gives me courage.[1]

What is so special about that statement of Gandalf's, hmmm? In case you are not well versed in either of the movie trilogies, Bilbo Baggins is a hobbit. Hobbits have some of the most ordinary, unexciting lives on the imaginary planet of J.R.R. Tolkien's Middle-earth. They are consumed with everyday matters of farming, eating, naps, and beer. They are homebodies who do not like adventure or traveling or anything unplanned, especially if it smells of danger. He is describing a very ordinary being as someone who gives him hope and courage. It is the very irony of this little hobbit who has taken on a terrific challenge of parading the countryside with a band of dwarves on a quest to kill a dragon and take back the dwarves' gold.

Back on planet earth, I would propose to you that many of us feel just like the hobbits. Our lives are filled with a house, a spouse, 2.5 kids, and a pet. Our worlds revolve around which holiday is approaching next, which new movie is playing at the theatre, which team is going to win the next championship . . . ordinary events.

But Gandalf dares to suggest something about Bilbo, about you, and about me. In this theater of the common, mundane events of our lives, grand stories are being lived out. Heroic acts of kindness and love are changing the world. Dragons are falling and treasures are being restored by people who are just walking steadily through their days! A stay-at-home mom, a salesman, a skilled worker, a roughneck in the oil field, a mechanic, a student, a teacher, doing everyday life the best they can, many times with extraordinary results.

Who you are matters! Who I am matters! OUR LIVES MATTER!

As you read this book, I want you to know that the life you are currently living is not small, insignificant, or wasteful. Instead, imagine that the Lord has been directing your steps. Imagine that you are directly in the center of where God has designed you to be. Imagine that the fate of our modern Middle-earth depends on you—the average, ordinary guy or girl

SCOTT DARYL ANDERSON

who does small acts of kindness, making the world a better place and keeping the darkest of evils at bay.

1

Unreal Expectations

What makes earth feel like hell is our expectation that it should feel like heaven.
—Chuck Palahniuk

A jaunt into any bookstore will give the most confident of readers an overload of reasons to be depressed. The ever-growing self-help aisle has guru after guru proclaiming that we should be more than we are, do more than we are doing, and achieve more than we are achieving. We are supposed to be a super-dad or super-mom, making more money than we can count, and enjoying a version of life that looks nothing like ours.

As I peruse the self-help section, questions begin to surge in my mind like: Is any of that reality? What really is the destiny of our lives? Is there really a magic formula or recipe that insures one will be a millionaire or a celebrity in five easy steps?

For most of us, life is boring compared to what our culture is screaming at us. Normal has been practically ridiculed, viewed as unwanted or not enough. An inherent danger lies in that line of thinking. I found this to be true recently while talking to one of my sons. He is approaching his mid-thirties and is beginning to reflect on his last ten years. He has begun to openly question whether or not he has wasted his life. He is married to a smart, Godly woman, and they have two beautiful kids. He is a coach at a charter school and makes a direct impact on kids' lives every day.

I was puzzled at his question and then frustrated and later downright angry. Not at him, but at a culture that would make someone with such a wonderful, beautiful life feel inadequate and lacking. My son's perspective was out of focus. His attention was on what he had not achieved or what he had not done rather than on how much God has blessed him and how many lives God has allowed him to impact. My son needed a paradigm shift, a new set of lenses from which to view his life through.

FINDING THE EXTRA IN YOUR ORDINARY

What Most People's Lives Look Like

In our world today, "average" is ridiculed and despised. Many books and conferences tell us how to rise above average and to be something more. People preach at themselves and look longingly into mirrors wishing they were not . . . average. We equate average with not working hard and a sense of mediocrity. But is that necessarily true?

The average people that I know are hardworking. They work diligently at their careers and spend thousands of dollars on continuing education to remain relevant in an ever-changing world. They work overtime, even missing their children's activities from time to time to put groceries on their tables. They love their families and give an inordinate amount of effort to making sure their families have all they need and most of what they want. Outside of the home, they give their time, their talents, and their treasure to the community, volunteering in different ways as they model good citizenship for their children.

Mediocre, they are not. (Excuse the Yoda'ism!)

The vast majority of people's lives look, well, normal. Work, school, practice, church, activities, a movie, eating out, Red Box, mowing the lawn, etc. We all have routines and schedules. We have demands that we must effectively prioritize in order to determine what must and SHOULD come first.

To listen to tabloid TV, news, and magazines, the lives of celebrities, athletes, and millionaires are far greater than the ordinary lives we lead. From dawn to sunset, we are bombarded with images and stories that lead us to believe those people are so special that we should follow their every move on Twitter or Instagram. This trend can even be felt inside the church. Pastors and evangelists are, at times, elevated to celebrity status as they are featured on TV shows and invited to conferences to speak to thousands. Most of these men and women are sincere and committed to Jesus and to the church; their messages are inspired, motivational, and even entertaining. However, for the majority of us on the other side of the pulpit, we have very little in common with these high-profile ministers of the Gospel.

If we adhere to the philosophy (or maybe propaganda) of the media, the subtle message is clear. Our lives just aren't that great. Somehow, our lives don't stack up or are not as interesting as the people in the limelight. *THEY* are special! *WE*, you and I, are average…Ordinary!

Why Our Culture Wants More

Touch-screens, apps, music, "smart" houses, Alexa, Siri, YouTube videos, and more videos. We live in a culture that rarely unplugs and is wired as if we are on life support. Today's economy is consumer driven; the more we have, the more we want. Technology is advancing so rapidly that the next new phone or app is available before we have mastered the previous one. Obsolescence has taken on an entirely new meaning.

The entire world is spending an enormous amount of time looking at screens tied to the internet and/or media. The chart below shows that we rank sixth worldwide in minutes of screen usage per day.[2]

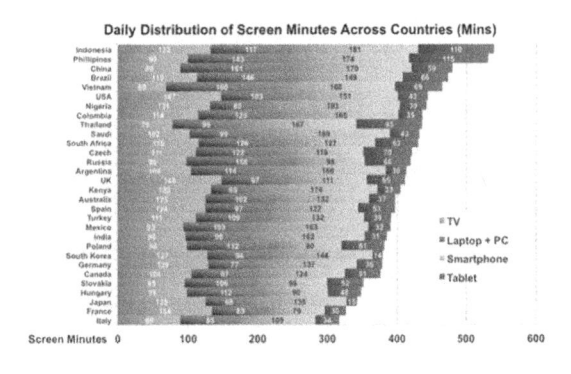

FINDING THE EXTRA IN YOUR ORDINARY

In a fast-paced, connected world, we are trading actual reality for virtual reality. While we are advancing in electronic connectivity, we are digressing in personal connectivity.

Our economy is being pushed to consume more and more all the time. With sophisticated ad campaigns come a perceived need and an ever-growing want to spend, spend, spend. With this pressure comes an ever increasing need to earn more money. However, there are a finite number of jobs that are at the top tier of wage earners. In fact, upper echelon jobs make up only 2 percent of wage earners in America according to the IRS.[3]

Americans are struggling to maintain a middle class existence on $60,000 or less for a family of four. The average American worker made $57,617 in 2016.[4] These numbers reveal a growing issue, causing concern and anxiety for consumers. More and more people don't feel like their money can put them where they want to be. With the pressure to keep up with those we are trying to impress, there is little wonder why people feel their lives are inadequate.

As you read this, you might be saying to yourself, "Not everyone is in that trap or situation. You don't have to have everything." True, but tell that to your eight-year-old who really, really wants to go to Disney World.

According to NerdWallet.com, in 2017, the average family carried $15,654 in credit card debt alone. Forty-one percent of those responding to the survey stated that their debt was a direct result of their purchasing unnecessary items above and beyond what their budgets could handle.[5]

Add a mortgage and a car payment or two into the equation and you get the idea. Reality paints a harsh picture, which is why I believe most people think their lives lack the luster that the "Jet-Set" have.

SCOTT DARYL ANDERSON

Have you seen a music video lately? They've become rare, but those still in existence typically portray a lavish party with people living an unrealistic lifestyle of fun fueled by drugs, alcohol, sex, and money. Sadly, today's culture can't distinguish between Hollywood scripts and reality. An inner city kid may watch a neighborhood gang-banger with cars, chains, *benjis* ($100 bills) and women; he sees the music video in living color. Of course, school would seem boring to that kid. Why study? Why spend time and sweat to play a sport? Street life looks like a fast track to success, yet teens fail to see that this lifestyle is also a quick way to end up in a pine box.

Conversely, a kid may live in a great neighborhood with a supportive family. He may go to a great high school, get a quality education, go to a four-year college of his choice, and earn a degree. After all that dedication and diligence, the graduate lands a less than fantastic job working a desk in a storage facility or as a cable guy (true examples, by the way). According to a CNN report, Goldman Sachs' projections for college graduates' landing quality jobs aren't looking great. Graduates of 2015 on average will not make enough money to break even until age thirty-one. Graduates of 2030 will break even at about thirty-three years of age, while 2050 graduates will likely have to wait until about age thirty-seven to start getting ahead.[6] How does one save for retirement? When does life begin to look positive with these projections?

In spite of all these ominous projections, I have good news. There is hope. What we need is a change in our perspective. Keep turning the page!

2

The Average Life of People

We're all torn between the desire for privacy and the fear of loneliness.
　　—Andy Rooney

SCOTT DARYL ANDERSON

*If we were good
at everything we
would have no need
for each other.*
—Simon Sineck

Salespeople, waiters and waitresses, carpenters, lawyers, mechanics, nurses, plumbers, teachers, soldiers, and doctors. This incomplete list names just a few of the wide range of career choices of many people. Purposely left off the list are celebrities, pro-athletes, CEOs of multinational corporations, and supermodels.

FINDING THE EXTRA IN YOUR ORDINARY

Millions of people are working diligently at seemingly ordinary jobs, but make no mistake. If you think these jobs are "ordinary," you're wrong. Let the air conditioner go out in your house in the middle of a hot, humid summer day in the South and you quickly realize how important the A/C guy really is. He is worth every penny to get that machine running again. After all, if Momma ain't happy, ain't nobody happy!

Our worlds are held together with the communal duct tape of all our average lives blended together. Countless services are given and used on a daily basis. Each one of these services is critical in keeping our homes in order, our conveniences flowing, and our lifestyles never missing a beat.

In movies, the attention is given to the "stars." However, without the production assistants, the special effects people, the stuntmen, and countless numbers of extras, the movie would not be as memorable or moving as the whole. And so it is with us. Each of our lives, regardless of the supporting role we play, is necessary in order for society to operate flawlessly.

FINDING THE EXTRA IN YOUR ORDINARY

What Is Truly Important

In the same vein, the world is filled with moms and dads, grandparents, cousins, friends, loved ones, mentors, pastors, and ministers. At times we take these people for granted; but when life gets interesting, weird, or downright out of control, these are the people who matter most. Celebrities are not who we call when someone is losing their battle with cancer. When the phone rings and someone dear to us has been downsized, pro athletes will not soothe the pain of the moment. Instead, the people who walk with us every day are the ones we turn to and lean on. These are the people we have given permission to speak into our lives, the ones we trust.

Many times we lose perspective not just of others, but of ourselves. Look at the housewife who feels like she has wasted her life just "raising kids." Or the husband and father who feels like his entire life is on eternal repeat: get up, go to work, come home, go to sleep, do it again tomorrow. Or the student who is up to his eyeballs in studying, writing papers, and taking exams while holding down a part-time job.

Are there any other roles so noble, so necessary? What the world has labeled "average," I would like to re-label as heroic. Life doesn't exist without people doing the ordinary on a daily basis. No greater hero exists than the soldier, be it male or female, who awakens everyday with the mission of protecting our country against all threats whether foreign or domestic. No one is doing more for society than the single parents who selflessly deny themselves so that their children can have much of what other kids have via a double-income home.

We must stop saying our lives do not matter that much. We are like a coral reef. Outwardly, life may look drab and dull . . . immovable. But life is created because that coral exists, life in vivid, living color with immeasurable species benefiting from its existence. What a great picture of how the mundane becomes miraculous.

Do you really think your child, your brother, or your friend wants anyone else at their big game, dance recital, graduation, or retirement party than you? They might be so bold as to even say it, but know this —they will be looking for your face in the crowd. You may be *THE* most important person to them and never even realize it.

Recently, I was visiting a dear friend. He is one of the first young men I have had the privilege to disciple in ministry. He has become a very successful worship leader, and I am very proud of him. He was sharing with me how his fourteen-year-old daughter, who is becoming womanly before his eyes, wanted him to attend her middle school's football games with her. He was busy at the church and typically exhausted when he got home. In his mind, the football game was a small thing, nothing to be taken seriously. After all, she wasn't even a cheerleader or band member, just a student. I looked at him in utter disbelief. I peered right into his eyes and said, "If you don't take her to the game, another boy will be delighted to." The look on his face was priceless. I followed up with this question, "How long do you think she is going to want you to take her to the big game?" He got it and got it immediately. These things are not small; they are enormous, possibly even galactic in scope. Those three hours could define for her how a man is supposed to treat her for a lifetime. Those brief hours could instill in her heart that she is the apple of her father's eye. Can any other task be more important in the atmosphere of our current culture?

Spending time with a spouse, a child, an aging parent—these are the important things of the ordinary life.

They are the concrete in the foundation of our lives. They are the stem cells of the relationships that matter most. In order for those relationships to form properly, they need to incubate in the nest of love and time spent with one another.

How to Balance Our Drive over Our Destiny

Destiny is a powerful word. *Webster's Dictionary* defines it as "a predetermined course of events often held to be an irresistible power or agency."[7] In common terms, destiny is life as it unfolds. We have designs, we make plans, and then life happens. We get married, have kids, start a job out of necessity, make mistakes, etc. Destiny is more akin to our well-meant designs blowing up in our faces. Thinking back on some of my personal disasters, I can attest that they have been some of my least favorite memories! Thankfully, after some time has passed, we typically realize how God used that very thing in our lives to shape us just the way He wants us.

God uses our most difficult moments to shape and form our destiny which conflicts with our overwhelming drive to succeed. Webster's defines drive as "the impetus to carry on or through energetically."[8] Our drive is what pushes us to excellence. It is the inner will to hold out hope against all odds that we can achieve whatever we put our minds to. Drive is a marvelous thing until it gets completely out of balance.

Our destiny is something we MUST accept while our drive is something we have to control. Have you ever met someone who simply was trying too hard? The individual presses so hard, even to the detriment of everyone around them. I am not referring to their work ethic here; that is a wonderful quality to possess. Instead, I am talking about someone who is obsessed with achieving and is willing to run over anyone or do whatever is necessary to attain his personal zenith. This person is oblivious to others like a tornado is to a town. This person's drive is out of balance and wreaks havoc on others. More times than not, this type of person hurts others, but, worse yet, he may not even be aware of the pain inflicted by his actions.

I once heard a great man say, "One of the worst things in life is to succeed at the wrong thing."[9] He was referring to a friend of mine who had become very successful in a career track that would eventually cost him his family, his job, and his character. My friend's drive was to be the very best at what he was doing while his destiny was to be a good husband, father, and minister. The good news is that my friend finally realized his error, and the man who said this about him became his personal mentor.

Our drive can create a great amount of energy inside us to do and achieve amazing things, but it must be balanced with a great sense of who God has made us to be—our destiny. If that gets out of balance, a person runs the risk of losing everything for the sake of his or her own desires to be "more" than they currently are.

Jesus told the parable of "a certain rich man yielded an abundant harvest." He harvested so much grain that his current silos were beyond capacity. "Then he said, 'This is what I'll do. I will tear down my barns and build bigger ones, and there I will store my surplus grain. And I'll say to myself, "You have plenty of grain laid up for many years. Take life easy; eat, drink and be merry." But God said to him, 'You fool! This very night your life will be demanded from you. Then who will get what you have prepared for yourself?'"[10]

Regrettably, there have been many people who have lost their souls and much more chasing after possessions and positions they thought would bring them great happiness. If our drive is centered on what God wants, then typically we will continue to keep our God-given destiny in focus. But when our drive is only about getting what we want and when we want it, then the outcome is usually quite disastrous.

Sadly, one group seems to get this wrong more so than many others—ministers. I have watched on more than one occasion a minister become so caught up in expanding his church that he misses the higher calling of being a fully engaged dad to his kids. We must never mistake great causes for the destiny that God has placed in our hands. We must be ever mindful of what He has called us to do, first and foremost. By placing our powerful drive squarely in the hands and purposes of God, we can rest peacefully knowing our destiny will also be secure.

3

Faithful in the Little

It's the little details that are vital. Little things make big things happen.
—John Wooden

SCOTT DARYL ANDERSON

A mountain is composed of tiny grains of earth. The ocean is made up of tiny drops of water. Even so, life is but an endless series of little details, actions, speeches, and thoughts. And the consequences whether good or bad of even the least of them are far-reaching.
—Swami Sivananda

FINDING THE EXTRA IN YOUR ORDINARY

Sometimes the hardest things to do are the things we do every day—the mundane, monotonous, routine, ordinary things that comprise our lives. My wife really struggles with living a life where the days seem to be identical copies of each other. Good or bad, she would rather see change all the time. At least that way, she knows that life is moving. Don't get me wrong; my wife is a master of the mundane. She just doesn't like it very much.

I, on the other hand, have a routine for everything. Eat, sleep, shower, work, write a blog article. I am pretty much going to do it the same every time. Confession—I once forgot to wash my hair in the shower because I was grimy from yard work and wanted to bathe my body first. Sad, huh? That one change threw me completely out of whack.

If you thought that was funny, wait till you realize that I can't stand to do routine, repetitious duties around the house while my wife doesn't like to make the broad, sweeping, decisions that incite the very change she so desires. We are a conundrum! But it works.

The reality is nothing happens without doing the smallest things first and doing them with your best effort. God has a law in the universe of first and best. You see it in the offerings of Cain and Abel in Genesis 4. Cain offered some of his produce after he enjoyed the first and best. Abel offered the first of his livestock's offspring, the very best.

Some people want to make this a big theological debate about a blood offering over the produce of the ground that Cain was trying to give the Lord. But God never had a problem with what Cain was offering; God had a huge problem that Cain offered what was left over after he had first enjoyed the very best for himself. In fact, God even tells him, "If you do what is right, your offering will be accepted."

I stunk at algebra. It scared me to death. Oh, I got the big topics. Invariably, I would foul up the little things! My nemesis was always incorrectly changing the signs on each side of the equation or forgetting to change them altogether. Take those same small mistakes into a checkbook and you can end up with insufficient fund notices coming out of your ears. Take that same issue into your job where maybe you are trusted with a lot of money for a company and everyone in the business can suffer dearly.

The fact is small details are critical to success. Most of the people who are running big businesses, organizations, or causes did not start out with a huge entity already in their hands. Most of them began very small and worked. Worked really hard. And then, worked some more, sometimes not seeing fruit for five, ten, or even twenty years. Then all of a sudden—BOOM! Their longtime efforts paid off huge.

Jesus said you won't be trusted with the big things until you are faithful in the little.[11] So how do we do that? By being a master of the mundane.

SCOTT DARYL ANDERSON

Being Consistent—Being the Master of the Mundane

Romans 12:1 is our key verse in this journey. I love the way it reads in The Message:

> So here's what I want you to do, God helping you: Take your everyday, ordinary life—your sleeping, eating, going-to-work, and walking-around life—and place it

> before God as an offering. Embracing what God does for you is the best thing you can do for him. (12)

God's message doesn't get much clearer than this, does it? Even God knows that much of your life is filled with the ordinary. But I know a secret. Psst, come close. I want to whisper this into your ear. He takes great joy in watching us do the everyday things in our lives. Just like us, He gets a real kick out of watching His kids.

I love to be in our house when our son has no idea we are watching him. He is busy playing with blocks or putting another stuffed animal in time out or developing even more super powers, and he has no idea that I am grinning from ear to ear watching him be himself.

We derive joy from that because our Creator does too. The idea that we have to achieve greatness, create a masterpiece, make millions of dollars or be the next Einstein in order to be loved is silly in the eyes of God. He made us exactly as He wanted us. He marvels in our existence just as much as we marvel in His!

I love the last part of verse 1: "Embracing what God does for you is the best thing you can do for him."

Simply embracing what God does for you and who He has made you to be is very best thing we can do for Him. The idea really isn't complicated. So, why is embracing the ordinary so difficult for us? Embracing means to give it a hug . . . to love it. Yet many of us simply despise the ordinary. On this side of Eden, we are not very good at "being." God didn't create human doings. He created human beings. But the truth is we struggle to "be." We know something is very, very wrong with us and we are always striving to fix our flaws. However, the fix is only found in Jesus Christ. By His stripes, we are healed and set free from ourselves.

Once we have accepted His incredible, amazing grace, a new goal comes into view—consistency. Getting free from ourselves gives us permission to be who God made us to be. Once we begin to live authentic lives, Romans 12:1 can be fulfilled. Our everyday, ordinary lives begin to connect with the life-giving embrace of a loving Father.

Practice being yourself all the time. I know that sounds strange, but we live in a world that is screaming at you to not be yourself. From the checkout aisles to any number of television shows available on cable or satellite, everything is telling you to dress this way, look that way, act this way, be like so-and-so. It makes me dizzy. Scream, "NO!" Be you . . . consistently.

I am no guru, but I do read and listen to one. His name is Jesus. He has given us marching orders that we must each work out in our daily walk. We must be intentional. We must incorporate the crucial concepts He has given us in order to discover the extra in our ordinary.

1. Start with the small tasks.

2. Give your very best effort—"offering."
3. Be your authentic self.

4

When God Puts His Extra into Your Ordinary

Will God ever ask you to do something you are not able to do? The answer is yes—all the time! It must be that

way, for God's glory and kingdom. If we function according to our ability alone, we get the glory; if we function according to the power of the Spirit within us, God gets the glory. He wants to reveal Himself to a watching world.
—Henry T. Blackaby, *Experiencing the Spirit: The Power of Pentecost Every Day*

FINDING THE EXTRA IN YOUR ORDINARY

> *Those in whom the Spirit comes to live are God's new Temple. They are, individually and corporately, places where heaven and earth meet.*
> —N. T. Wright, *Simply Christian: Why Christianity Makes Sense*

Since the fall of mankind in Genesis 3, nothing has been more important to God than to restore the relationship of His Spirit with our humanity. The God of the universe wanted His creation to know the sheer joy of His indwelling Spirit inside us. The same fellowship that the Father, the Son, and the Holy Spirit experience was His goal for us also. God in us!

All of recorded history was destined to arrive at the climax of John 20 and Acts 2 when the very Spirit of Christ Himself dwelt in our mortal bodies. No longer were temples and special rooms necessary. Gone were the days of intermediaries in special robes making sacrifices on behalf of the people. Instead, God began meeting us right where we are and moving directly inside of us—true relationship.

When the Spirit of God meets human flesh, extraordinary things begin to erupt. Peter, the crusty fisherman who had a knack for arguing with Jesus face to face, is likely uneducated (Acts 4:13) and even needed John Mark to record his remembrances of Christ while He was here on the earth. Peter, the man who publicly denied Jesus three times after promising Him just hours before that he would go to the cross with Him if necessary, becomes a great leader, healer, teacher, and apostle.

How does God promote a guy with that kind of resumé? How does Peter assume this fantastic life with all sorts of heroic stories, even being crucified upside down? Simple, the ordinary man accepted the extraordinary Spirit to fill him and rest on him. God really doesn't make this difficult. If you ask the Father to give you His Spirit—He will!

> If you then, though you are evil, know how to give good gifts to your children, how much more will your Father in heaven give the Holy Spirit to those who ask Him! (Lk 11:13)

FINDING THE EXTRA IN YOUR ORDINARY

The Bible is filled with a litany of ordinary men and women who put their trust in the Lord and allowed His Spirit to do unbelievable and extraordinary actions.

> Joseph, whose dreams were shattered while stuck in a dungeon after being falsely accused of rape, becomes the leader of Egypt second only to Pharaoh. Genesis 37-45.

Tamar seduced her father-in-law, Judah, but is in the lineage of Jesus. Genesis 38

Gideon, who had an epic poor self-image, led his three hundred men to miraculous victory. Judges 6-7

Samson, who never honored one part of his vow to God, was empowered with superpower-like strength to literally crush the Philistines. Judges 13-15

Deborah, a female judge, led the armies of Israel to victory. Judges 4

David, the guy who had an affair and killed his lover's husband, took down Goliath with the tools of a sheep herder. 1 Samuel 17

Elijah, whose emotions had a tendency to roller-coaster, defeated the four hundred prophets of Baal. 1 Kings 18

Elisha, Elijah's protégé, raised the Shunammite's son from the dead. 2 Kings 4

Daniel, abducted and taken to Babylon to be made a servant,

spent a night with the lions. Daniel 6.

Hananiah, Mishael and Azariah (Shadrach, Meshach and Abednego), were made to be eunuchs, given new identities directly opposed to God and trained for a pagan king's service, yet were saved while in the furnace. Daniel 2

Peter, the hot-headed disciple who denied Christ three times, healed the crippled man at the Temple. Acts 3

Stephen, considered to be a great guy like lots of other people, while being stoned to death for his faith in Christ, saw Jesus standing at the right hand of the Father. Acts 7

> Paul, the Christian killer, was converted, used to bring about many miracles, wrote much of the New Testament and led the Roman world to Christ. Acts 9-28

All these remarkable acts were authored by God's Spirit at work inside of these common people. They were no more extraordinary than you or I. These believers, by faith, were willing to allow His Spirit to move through them and accomplish only what God could do. They were a conduit of His power and active presence in each circumstance.

I began this chapter with Peter and that is where I want to wrap it up. Peter was indeed brash and impulsive. He had a tendency to misunderstand his place even in the presence of God incarnate. He could be a little thick-headed and stubborn. But he also was the only disciple to step out of the boat and walk on water at Jesus's invitation. Did he deny Jesus three times? Yes, but that took place at the Temple where Jesus was being tried by the high priest and Sanhedrin. Other than John, Peter was the only disciple in close proximity to Jesus after His arrest, knowing all the while that he, too, might be arrested.

Peter had his shortcomings, but he was also a man of profound faith. His first real encounter with Jesus changed his life forever. He had fished all night. He was tired, sore, and angry because he and his crew had not caught any fish. When your livelihood depends on catching, you are not a happy camper when you only go fishing. He is cleaning and tending to his nets as Jesus approaches and asks if He can use Peter's boat as a platform from which He can teach the crowd.

Sure. Why not? Get in. (Because I am certainly not selling fish today!)

The message is nice. There is true life in this man's words. I like Him a lot. "I am sorry, what was that?"

Jesus, "Let's shove out for a catch."

I have often wondered what type of mental gymnastics were going on inside of Peter's head. People who are usually good at something rarely want to take advice from novices. I can hear the conversation inside Peter's heart: "Hey, bud, why don't you stick to teaching and let me worry about the fishing?"

To Peter's credit, when he opened his mouth it was graceful. "Sure, yeah, okay. Ummm, we can do that . . . I guess."

You know the rest of this story. The catch was huge. It even began swamping the boat. In this moment, Peter's faith was birthed. Jesus had just supplied all His needs in the world while also exposing the greatest need of his heart all in one miraculous catch of fish. Peter's response is telling. "Depart from me, Lord, for I am a sinful man." But the Spirit inside Jesus called to Peter's destiny, "From now on, you will catch men."

It would happen again, when Jesus and the boys were taking a break at the spa town of Caesarea-Philippi.

Jesus is giving them a pop quiz and they don't even know it. "Who do men say that I am?" The responses were varied. The real test question came off of Jesus's tongue and hung in the air like a fog. "Who do YOU say that I am?" (Emphasis added.)

The question is a line in the sand. They have been witnessing the miracles and listening to His teachings but now is the moment of truth, the time to make a real decision.

And who would speak up? None other than Peter. "You are the Christ, the Son of the Living God!" Peter may have been short on brains, but not on faith. Peter has been sold on the true nature and identity of Jesus since that day in the boat while wading through water and fish and scales and slime.

Once again, the Spirit of God through Jesus speaks to Peter's destiny, "On this Rock, I will build my church."

So, it's not a stretch for Peter when he hears Jesus say, "Greater works will you do in my name." Peter is quick to trust what the Lord says and to begin acting on it immediately. This is what life led by the Spirit is all about. Just listening to God and acting upon His leading, just having the faith of a child. A kid hears his dad say, "Jump to me!"

The child, trusting his dad, never blinks, never thinks his dad won't catch him. That is how we should be when the Spirit speaks.

My wife and I have personally witnessed this in our marriage and life. God has routinely shown Himself faithful and even miraculous when we put our hope and trust in Him. Too much month at the end of the money and, bam, money is given to us without asking. Praying over a woman's leg and seeing it grow, eliminating her back pain. Witnessing one of my students pray over a classmate who struggled with migraine headaches and seeing her healed. On and on it goes, all these are examples of life by the Spirit.

When God touches you, speaks to you, moves you, makes you feel compelled to share the hope you have in Jesus with others, it is life by the Spirit, full and active, vivid and alive. Life is never boring. The Holy Spirit can take your average, ordinary, mundane existence and make it power-filled, life-giving, and supernatural.

God never wants to just change you. Instead, through you, He wants to change the world around you, the world in which you reside as a dad or mom, coach or teacher, doctor or nurse, boss or worker. By infusing you with the same power that raised Christ from the dead, He wants to transform everything and everyone around you, powerfully, even miraculously.

5

Faithful in the Big

Patience is necessary, and one cannot reap immediately where one has sown.
—Saruman Kierkegaard

You cannot hold on to anything good. You must be continually giving— and getting. You cannot hold on to your seed. You must sow it— and reap anew. You cannot hold on to riches. You must use them and get other riches in return.
—Robert Collie

October 7, 1950? No one will likely shout out the answer to the question correctly, but that is the date that

FINDING THE EXTRA IN YOUR ORDINARY

Mother Teresa began her Missionaries of Charity in Calcutta with twelve members. A meager start for such a spiritual colossus, but a seed planted rarely remains small. At the time of her death, Missionaries of Charity consisted of 4,500 plus religious sisters (nuns). This worldwide ministry reaches those who are refugees, former prostitutes, the mentally ill, sick children, abandoned children, lepers, people with AIDS, and the aged. Since her death the Catholic Church has given her saint status which is no small thing. Her face is immediately recognizable around the world.

Now that is an impressive list for one Godly woman. When she began, do you think she had a clue what God would do with her simple willingness? Do you honestly think she was expecting to speak in front of world leaders and to make an impact anywhere other than the ghettos of India?

When the Little Becomes Big

Sometimes the thing God has you doing that seems so very ordinary will in fact become bigger than you ever dreamed. For most people who want their lives to mean more than the daily routine, they begin with something small, a personal passion birthed deep inside their heart. Something that is bigger than themselves, but something that parallels their daily, weekly, and even monthly normal. Look at the areas of your life that you are most passionate about. The activities that you love to do is a great place to begin because God has placed that set of likes and dislikes in you for a reason . . . a purpose.

I have a friend who loves hunting and is extremely good at it. Hunting is his passion. One day while hunting, God interrupted his entire day, "Jeff,

I want you to take kids hunting that will never be able to go on their own." Jeff was not argumentative at all and responded to God with a willing heart.

Having no clue as to how to begin, he went to a hospital and asked if they had any terminally ill or extremely sick kids who would like to go hunting? The hospital asked him to meet with their board to get a better understanding of exactly what the activity would entail. He walked into the meeting wearing camo. Everyone else was in dresses, suits, ties, dress shoes—you know—civilized. The board still had not fully processed what Jeff wanted to do for these kids. He explained that he was going to take them into the woods and allow them to kill a deer . . . dead. "With a gun?" the board asked. Jeff responded confidently, "Yeah, that's how it's done." To his amazement, they said, "Why, yes, yes, we do have kids that would love that!"

And just like that, Jeff Warren's Dream Hunt Foundation was birthed. The first year he took just two or three kids. Those hunts were so successful that word began to spread. The next year the two or three kids turned into more than twenty. In the 2016–2017 season, he took ninety-seven. Dream Hunt had planned to take closer to 125, but the devastating rains in South

Louisiana derailed his weekend in the Baton Rouge area.

Jeff's foundation has been a great success but can also be a logistics nightmare. First of all, how does he take that many kids hunting? Well, he doesn't anymore. He quickly realized that nothing great happens without help. A lot of help!

Jeff has attracted a host of volunteers to help him bring about his Dream Hunt Weekends. It is beautiful thing to see how many people have jumped into the vision of what the Lord dropped into Jeff's big heart. He facilitates the properties and the guides that go along with each child. Jeff even recruits a volunteer videographer to record the entire event for the children to enjoy for the rest of their lives. He also has to provide a customized way for each hunter to get into a hunting blind uniquely set up for them, not to mention the hurdle of how the child will actually aim a gun and pull the trigger. Some of these children do not have great strength or the ability to manipulate the equipment. The foundation has to come up with rather creative ways for each child to be successful in the hunt.

I love what Jeff said when we talked about all of this. He grinned and said to me, "God isn't going to call you to something without providing everything you need." In fact, every need has always been fulfilled.

The smiles on the kids' faces during these weekends are enough to make anyone shout for joy and cry a river all at the same time.

Destiny and the Devil Is in the Details

All too often, the very thing that makes something extraordinary is the details. The smallest details can make an experience, an event, or even a vision very ordinary or propel it into a memory that lasts a lifetime. Not being redundant here, but doing your best in the smallest things typically results in an amazing big thing.

For the Dream Hunt Foundation and Jeff Warren, you can imagine that the list of details is long. Many man hours go into pulling off a hunt for a child with special needs. Jeff is trying to deliver a defining moment for these kids on every trip he puts together.

In addition to affecting children with disabilities or special needs, these weekends also impact Jeff's family. What kind of a job allows someone to be gone so much? How does he spend time with his own children? How does he balance the ordinary with something like this?

I asked Jeff how does he make all of this work? His answer was quick and decisive. "My wife has been the most amazing person in this entire journey. She gets that this really isn't about me. She has never once nagged me about the weekends spent giving these kids the hunt of their lives." Not only is she incredibly supportive, but she is also tackling two roles on the homefront while he is doing what God has called him to do.

6

The Greatest of These Is Love

*Children spell
love T-I-M-E.*
—Dr. Anthony
 P. Witham

SCOTT DARYL ANDERSON

It is not a lack of love, but a lack of friendship that makes unhappy marriages.
—Friedrich Neitzsche

If you want to change the world, go home and love your family.
—Mother Teresa

Many times, the most precious people in our lives are the ones who get forgotten in the midst of our doing great things. How do we balance the two paradigms of ordinary and extraordinary?

Love Is Spelled T-I-M-E

A hard truth in life is that it doesn't matter how much you say you love someone. They really only know you love them when you prioritize them with your time. Time is a currency of sorts. Interestingly, we speak of time by using accounting terms. You spend, save, invest, and waste time. All of these are exactly the same words we use to describe money. Make no mistake, you are living with excellent accountants who observe how you spend your time, and whether it is with them or in other ways. There are many wonderful, even extraordinary things to attach yourself to in this world. But the real question here isn't what is worthy of your time? Even if what you are giving your time to is extraordinary, you still have to ask the question: Have I been called to this?

Remember, those little feet running through your house or apartment only understand one thing: you are or are not spending time with them. Are your causes so earth-shattering that you are willing to miss time with your own kids, time you can never redeem?

Like money, once time is spent, it's spent. No returns, no refunds. It's just gone.

The wife or husband, brother or sister, best friend or confidante, are they worth more than a meeting, a makeover, or even a mission? You had better be called by God Almighty to whatever has your attention when you are not engaged with the ones who mean the most to you.

Even then, there must be balance in how you spend this currency called time.

SCOTT DARYL ANDERSON

Do They Know?

I know this all too well. I grew up in the 1970s and '80s. I had much older siblings, so I was essentially an only child with two brothers and a sister. My dad was retired from the Air Force for the majority of my years in school. After retiring, he made great money and was a diligent, hard-working man. He is what many men pride themselves on being—a provider. We enjoyed the benefits of that provision. We had a pool in the back yard most of my life. I was always allowed to play Little League football and basketball through our local YMCA and to go to children and youth camps through my church.

My dad loved to fish. We always had a boat and I was privileged enough to go with him to Toledo Bend, Caddo Lake, and other local places. We fished! There is no better way for a young person to grow up than outside in my opinion. Ahh, the adventure of it all. Camping in the back of the truck. Eating beanie-weenies out of the can. Smelling like mosquito repellant for days.

My father was a very quiet man. His display of love was to provide and to take me fishing. I, on the other hand, wanted more than anything to be told that I was loved by my dad. I had a need for people to verbalize their feelings toward me. Needless to say, this was a conundrum. He was displaying love the only way he knew how while I was desiring a display of love that he may never have been shown or taught during his own childhood.

From that, I grew up believing he did not love me, when in truth is, he did and still does. He just didn't know how to communicate it in a way that I could see it clearly. Imagine two people who speak two different languages with no interpreter. The situation can be wrought with confusion and mistrust. However, if enough time is spent working through the relationship, then the message does become clear and is not lost in translation.

As a teen, I really didn't know if my dad loved me due to his lack of verbalizing his feelings. As a man, I know he loves me because of the time we spent back then in a boat or in the woods. He invested his most precious commodity—time. In fact, he spent that time with me in his personal oasis—fishing.

Sidenote: We should all strive to communicate love in a way that will be received and comprehended by those who are most valuable in our lives. Be willing to continue a process of learning and growing so that the ones you love have exclamation points instead of question marks. Gary Chapman's bestseller *The Five Love Languages* is a great place to start.

In closing this chapter, many things in life demand our attention and time. Most are replaceable, while your family is not! Our highest priority should be the WHO and not the WHAT!

7

It's Who You Build, Not What You Build

Ordinary people can make an extraordinary impact on their own world.

—John Maxwell,
John Maxwell
Twitter Feed

The purpose of human life is to serve and to show compassion and the will to help others.
—Albert Schweitzer

Therefore if you have any encouragement from being united with Christ, if any comfort from his love, if any common sharing in the

Spirit, if any tenderness and compassion, then make my joy complete by being like-minded, having the same love, being one in spirit and of one mind. Do nothing out of selfish ambition or vain conceit. Rather, in humility value others above yourselves, not looking to your own interests but each of you to the interests of the others. (Phil. 2:1–4, NIV)

I have a friend named Larry who loves to ask me if I would like a cup of coffee. Now, Larry knows I hate coffee. He asks me just so I will turn him down . . . again and again and again. When I tell him no thanks, without fail Larry immediately says, "That's why nobody likes you, Scott." With friends like Larry, who needs any enemies, right? He once told me he wanted to encourage me. I was feeling a bit defeated and I suppose he picked up on that sentiment. So, knowing our typical conversation, I said, "Go for it." Larry's sense of humor did not disappoint. He said, "We are all dying right now." At the time, I could have thought of many things I wanted to say to Larry, but what he said is profoundly accurate.

No, no, don't throw the book across the room, please. I have a point. We should live as if we are aware, cognizant and attentive to the fact that we are headed towards our death. The clock is ticking on you and me right now as you are reading this. The sands of time are running through the hour glass, and a moment is coming when our life on earth will be over.

Nothing will give you a greater sense of living than knowing you are dying. I love the country song "Live like You Were Dying" by Tim McGraw that screams this same message. Taking time with those we love most takes less effort when you have the perspective that our lives are short and our moments are few.

What will really stand the test of time when your time is up? What will be left? The house that you have given many dollars to maintain? Maybe a business that you have spent more time building than you care to admit? The reality is that most of our earthly possessions get sold and split up among our heirs. Kids rarely continue a business their parents built over many years or live in the same house they grew up in when their parents pass on.

The Pyramids of Egypt are some of the most amazing structures left from antiquity, but no one has a clue who built them. Sad, right?

I ended the last chapter with the statement it's the who, not the what. What truly lasts is whatever you have invested into others. The love, the laughs, the tears, the memories, the moments, the firsts, the lasts, the days, hours, minutes and seconds you invested into OTHERS!

In this, our final chapter, I want to focus on the Apostle Paul. Paul was a true Renaissance man. He was well traveled, well studied, a businessman, a theologian, a missionary, a church planter, a worker of miracles. He wrote two-thirds of the New Testament, but I would humbly submit to you that his greatest achievement was not the amazing list I have just given you. Instead, it was the people that Paul invested in, people like Silas, Luke, Timothy, Apollos, Titus, Philemon, Phoebe, Andronicus, and Junia, Lucius, Jason, Sosipater, Epaphroditus, Urbanus, Clement, Aristarchus, Demas, and Tychicus. These men and women lasted, remained, kept going, and finished the work Paul started. They are his lasting legacy.

To read the end of one of Paul's letters is to step into a deep relationship of wishing people warm and loving farewells, see-you-soons, and send-all-of-my-love. The feeling is like watching military men and women reuniting with their loved ones at the airport after they have been deployed to a war zone. In those moments, those people are life itself. They ARE the extra in our ordinary lives.

For Paul, all the miles, miracles, jail cells, beatings, and salvations were really wrapped up in the people in those towns stretched out from Palestine and Asia Minor to the provinces of Roman. The people made it all worthwhile. In the end, these very people carried his legacy forward.

Your investment into your son or daughter, the time spent with your spouse or aging parent—it's the people in your life that will be the true trophies of our lives. When we arrive at the moment of our passing, these are the people whom you and I will want near us, wishing us well, giving us those last hugs, sweet kisses, and fond farewells. Even as I write this, the tears are flowing freely . . . as they should be.

When my mother went to be with the Lord in the spring of 2015, our long-time family pastor, Bro. Billy Pierce, officiated her funeral. He said something that day I will never forget. "All the things that made Mom so special to you and the children in life are the same things that make it hurt so much in her passing." My mother had impacted me. She had deposited into my heart, mind, and soul. And although I was hurting at the time, I knew then and I know now that she is not that far away from me.

Know this: the next time you look into the face of one of your kids or your spouse or a family member or a dear friend . . . you are really looking at someone in whom you have invested your entire life. Your character, integrity, beliefs, convictions, humor, and stories are being deposited into their hearts. Everything that God has placed inside of your heart should be passed on to them.

Contentment

I am not saying this because I am in need, for I have learned to be content whatever the circumstances. I

FINDING THE EXTRA IN YOUR ORDINARY

> *know what it is to be in need, and I know what it is to have plenty. I have learned the secret of being content in any and every situation, whether well fed or hungry, whether living in plenty or in want. I can do all this through him who gives me strength.*
> —Philippians 4:11–13 (NIV)

The real trick to finding the extra in your ordinary, everyday, right now life is contentment. Once again, everything in our culture is screaming that our lives should be more. Get more, be more, earn more, have more, buy more . . . but it's never enough. In the hit musical, *The Greatest Showman*, the character Jenny Lind sings a powerful song that summarizes our culture,

> All the shine of a thousand spotlights
> All the stars we steal from the night sky
> Will never be enough
> Never be enough
> Towers of gold are still too little

> These hands could hold the world but it'll
> Never be enough
> Never be enough

With desire like that, can a heart ever find peace?

Merriam-Webster defines *contentment* as "pleased and satisfied; not needing more." Life can throw things at you and me that can cause us to desire more. I, too, know the pain of heartache. I have saved this moment in the book to share with you my personal story. I pray it blesses you.

SCOTT DARYL ANDERSON

Growing up, I was athletic. I was a starter for all of my sports teams in football, basketball, and baseball. I was fortunate enough to be selected to a few all-star teams along the way. But, as most of you know all too well, life can be a bit of a roller-coaster ride.

As I hit those awkward teen years from seventh to ninth grade, I noticed I was not advancing athletically as well as I should. My orthodontist, Dr. Cope, also noticed that some of his treatment over the past two years for a slight overbite had totally reverted. His son and I had been friends, and I had played ball against him since Little League. Dr. Cope invited us to a consultation where he revealed his concerns. My mom and I went through a battery of doctors trying to get to the cause of the issue. What eventually came to light was devastating. At age fifteen, I was diagnosed with FSH muscular dystrophy. Dr. Woo at the muscular dystrophy clinic at the famed LSU Medical Center in Shreveport took just five minutes to diagnose me. I was devastated. At age fifteen, all my hopes and dreams were smashed against the hard reality that my body was beginning to and would continue to fail me. It was the summer between my freshman and sophomore years in high school.

What would people think? How would my friends react? Even more concerning was how would I react?

I don't remember much of my sophomore year of high school. It was a dark time for me. I was fearful that everyone was "noticing" my situation. My identity had always been an athlete, but I wasn't that any longer. I was insecure. I would have gladly welcomed some ordinary right about then. I was anything but content!

I had accepted Jesus as my Lord and Savior at age ten and had faithfully attended church even though my family rarely went. I felt betrayed by God with the revelation of FSH muscular dystrophy. How could a loving God do this to one of his kids? I was so hurt and so angry.

I would go to church and sit on the pew in a fog, numb to the world around me, hostile to my own negative thoughts about myself, and fearful that others were thinking the same negative thoughts. I mostly sat there minding my own business but not really entering into what the Spirit was doing. I knew I needed help and had no idea who or where to turn. So I did what my family had always done. I fished.

Fishing became my therapy. There was a bayou a short walk from our home. I spent many afternoons on the banks of that bayou catching bass and having some loud, angry talks with the Lord that were more truthfully described as AT the Lord.

What is so cool about Jesus is that He can handle those moments that we have. He just stood there with me and let me get out all of the venom that the discovery of this disease had created in me.

One Sunday, I was in church, minding my own business as usual. I was reading my Bible while the aforementioned Bro. Billy Pierce was preaching a sermon when the Lord did a miracle in me. He very patiently and lovingly whispered into my heart that He knew I was hurt by the loss of my dreams. But if I would take the dreams He had for me as my own, then He would be with me and bless me. Although I felt like this offer was more like an offer from the movie *The Godfather* ("I'm going to make him an offer he can't refuse.") I mean, how was I going to say no? I knew that Jesus was gently asking me to trust Him and that He meant every word.

From that moment on, I began to truly walk with God in a way I never had before. My relationship with the Lord became personal and vibrant. The Lord did amazing work in my heart. I got to a place where I could accept that the Lord was going to use what was happening in my body for His glory.

My youth minister back then was a baseball guy, Eddie Pentecost. He and his wife, Joyce, invested vast quantities of time in me. They were firm and loving. They guided me while also allowing me space to work through some tough issues. Eddie showed me how to really read the Bible and to walk with God.

These two very special people were responsible for my growth in the Lord. Without them, I likely wouldn't have survived these difficult years.

Amazingly, a day finally came when I was content with my body. I didn't just accept my circumstances, I owned them. My physical weakness became a place of confidence for me. On the backdrop of my ever-increasing physical weakness, God was painting a picture of strength and confidence.

I began doing some evangelism while in college. Once I finished college, I began traveling and speaking full time. The Lord allowed my story to impact many young people, and, for that, I am forever grateful.

However, life is full of little quirks. I was not at all content with the size or scope of my ministry. I had evangelist friends who were much busier than I was. I was being invited to the same churches year after year while they were touring the country. I was jealous!

Now God has a marvelous sense of humor. When I was a teen, I hated school. So what does He have me do next? That's right—teaching! I was looking for the exit at every opportunity. I looked for "better" jobs . . . anything but teaching!

Ironically, only when I had been replaced by someone who was certified did I realize the ministry that I had just lost. I had no idea how contented I was as a teacher until I wasn't one any longer.

One of the many things I love about Jesus is that if you fail a test, He makes you take it again. So six years later, I was given another opportunity to teach and I have been there ever since. I feel at home and love to interact with my students. Beyond a shadow of a doubt, teaching is the greatest youth ministry I have ever had.

Now one thing is for certain: nothing could get more ordinary than teaching. Same schedule every day. Same kids every day. Same lessons twice a year. To the casual observer, teaching might seem boring and mundane. But, because I am content in this God-given purpose, my career is extraordinary!

I have had thousands of kids come through my classroom. Many students have accepted Jesus in my class. Some make eternal decisions to walk with Him well into their adulthood. Teaching is anything but ordinary. I am on the front lines fighting for the souls of kids on a daily basis.

Perspective is the key. If you are struggling with being content in your job or your marriage, sit down and begin to write out all the reasons you are thankful for them. Allow the joy of the Lord to fill that job or relationship. Celebrate it, romance it, and pursue it with passion because you have no idea the rewards you are storing up for yourself in heaven. Get a new perspective. Be transformed by the renewing of your mind. (Romans 12:2)

Your life is more extraordinary than you know. Remember how I said that I was jealous of my ministry friends? One of them challenged me by telling me, "Your greatest sermon is just walking up to the podium." I knew what he was talking about. Walking had become difficult for me at the time he spoke that bit of truth. I had no idea of the magnitude of what God had done in my body and the testimony of God's strength and grace that was being revealed to everyone around me.

My ordinary, as it turns out, was extraordinary to everyone else . . . and so is yours!

Aftermath

I pray that through this book, you realize that your life means more than maybe you have ever imagined. I hope that God's personal message that you are necessary has been received. You may be a hobbit, but without you, the victory will not be won.

Never be ashamed of your life as long as you are spending it well in the eyes of God. It doesn't really matter what anyone else thinks anyway.

Take courage, my friend. Dare to live your life well. Hold your head high and be the person God has called you to be.

His,
Scott Daryl Anderson

Endnotes

[1] Jackson, Peter, dir. *The Hobbit*. 2012; :Metro-Goldwyn-Mayer,.
[2] Epstein, Zach. "Horrifying Chart Reveals How Much Time We Spend Staring at Screens Each Day." BGR, Boy Genius Report, url = bgr.com/2014/05/29/smart-phone-computer-usage-884 study-chart
[3] Jackson, Brooks. "Americans Making More than $250,000." FactCheck.org. April 20 2008. www.factcheck.org/2008/04/americans-making-more-than-250000.

[4] Household, Income. "US Household Income." Department of Numbers, 27 Feb. 2018, https://www.deptofnumbers.com/income/us/

[5] Issa, Erin El. "NerdWallet's 2017 Household Debt Study." *NerdWallet* (blog), March 4, 2018. www.nerdwallet.com/blog/credit-card-data/average-credit-card-debt-household.

[6] Long, Heather. "The Case Against Going to College." CNNMoney, Cable News Network, 9 Dec. 2015, money.cnn.com/2015/12/09/news/economy/college-not-worth-it-goldman.

[7] Webster, Miriam. "Destiny." Merriam-Webster. Accessed May 03, 2018. http://www.merriam-webster.com/dictionary/destiny?src=search-dict-box.

[8] Webster, Miriam. "Drive." Merriam-Webster. Accessed May 03, 2018. http://www.merriam-webster.com/dictionary/drive.

[9] Duron, Denny

10. NIV Bible. Https://Www.biblegateway.com/Passage/?Search=Luke+12&Version=NIV. Biblica, 2011, www.biblegateway.com/passage/?search=Luke+12&version=NIV. Luke 12:13-21
11. Luke 16:10. The Holy Bible.
12. Romans 12:1. The Holy Bible.

About the Author

Scott Daryl Anderson is a high school Bible teacher who has had a passion for young people since 1988. In 2015, with the help of a dedicated board, he launched Handicapped Outdoors, a 501c3 nonprofit that helps people with disabilities get back in the field and on the water in their pursuit of the great outdoors.

A devoted husband and father, Scott is available to speak at your next event. You can contact him at handicappedoutdoors@gmail.com or follow him at https://www.facebook.com/handicappedoutdoors.

CPSIA information can be obtained
at www.ICGtesting.com
Printed in the USA
LVHW090458120419
613944LV00001B/9/P